My Webkinz™ Companion Guide

Name_____

By Kathy Cothran

Dedicated to my friend Cheryl Boes who listens to all of my
ideas and helps me know when I have a good one!

I also thank my daughters for drawing the pictures used
throughout the book, and for helping me understand how
some of the games and activities work!
-Kathy

ISBN 978-1434894618

Visit our websites:
http://webkinzintheclassroom.com/
(is not an official site and is unaffiliated with GANZ)
http://turningtoysintotools.com/

A portion of all proceeds are donated to the Mark Victor Hansen
Literacy to End Poverty Foundation

Contents

Contents Continued

My Pets

Pet's Name	Type of Animal	Birthday	Favorite Things (Found in Your Pet's Biography)

And More of My Pets

Pet's Name	Type of Animal	Birthday	Favorite Things (Found in Your Pet's Biography)

And EVEN More
of My Pets

Pet's Name	Type of Animal	Birthday	Favorite Things (Found in Your Pet's Biography)

KinzCash ™ Recording

The amount of KinzCash™ that you have allows you to purchase all kinds of items for your pets. Some, such as food, are necessities, and others are just for entertainment! Each day when you log in, jot down in the chart how much KinzCash™ you start with. Then, just before you log out for the session, jot down how much KinzCash™ you have left. Sometimes you will have more than you started with by earning while you were engaged in the activities. Other times you will have less than you started with because you purchased items. Record the main reason for the difference in amounts. Being conscious of your money and how you spend it will help you be an aware consumer in real life!

Date	Starting KinzCash™ Amount	Ending KinzCash™ Amount	Difference in Amounts	Reason for the difference in amounts

Date	Starting KinzCash™ Amount		Difference in Amounts	Reason for the difference in amounts

Date	Starting KinzCash™ Amount	Ending KinzCash™ Amount	Difference in Amounts	Reason for the difference in amounts

Make Me Love Your Pet!

Write a descriptive paragraph about your favorite pet. Make your pet come alive for us so that all that read about your pet wish that the pet was theirs!

_____

_____

_____

_____

_____

_____

_____

_____

_____

_____

_____

_____

_____

_____

_____

_____

_____

_____

Draw your pet here!

Charting the Health, Happiness, and Hunger of Your Pet

A line graph is used to show change over time. The health, happiness, and hunger of your pet is something that changes over time. When you first log into Webkinz™ check on the status of your pet. Use one chart for each pet you will track. Connect the dots between each entry to show the change over time. Use a different color pencil for each category (health, happiness, and hunger.) Be sure to label the x and y axis of the chart!

Pet's Name_____

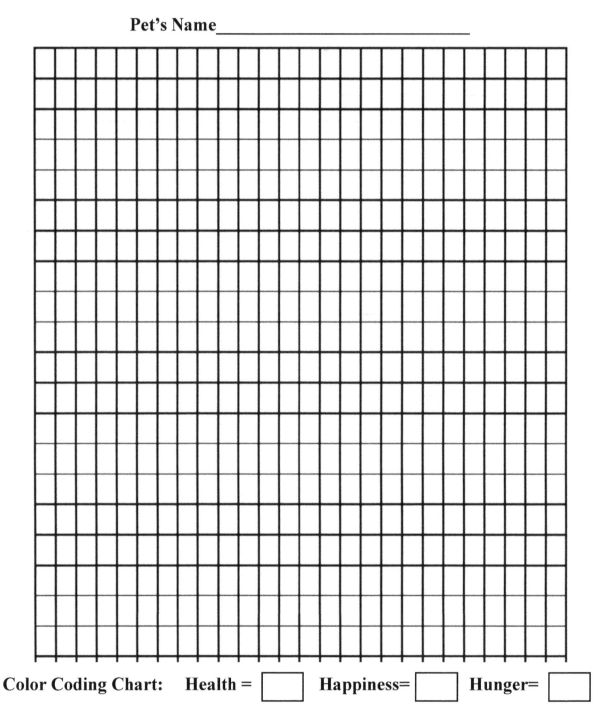

Color Coding Chart: **Health =** [ ]   **Happiness=** [ ]   **Hunger=** [ ]

Mapping Your Living Space

Your pets each have their own room and then you can purchase other rooms for them to enjoy, such as a backyard, bathroom, or general rooms. Draw the map of your living space that you created within Webkinz™ world below. Be specific for each room including where your pet sleeps, and any other details of the rooms. Also note where the doors are to go between rooms.

Mapping Your Living Space
And Giving Directions

Now that you have mapped your living space, you are going to have a party and invite all of your friends' pets to attend!

Pick a room to be your starting point, and then give directions, step by step, so that your friends can find you. Be sure to include, right, left, forward, behind, etc. These specific directions will enable your friends to find the right spot on the first try!

_____

_____

_____

_____

_____

_____

_____

_____

_____

_____

_____

_____

_____

_____

_____

_____

_____

_____

_____

Improving Your Typing Skills Using Lunch Letters

Billy the Goat is responsible for keeping the cafeteria clean. You must use the keyboard and type the falling letters before they hit the ground. This will improve your typing skills. Keep track of your scores on this log sheet so you can watch your typing skills and speed improve!

Date	Level #	Game Words per Minute	Game Characters per minute	Cumulative Accuracy:	Total Errors

Quizzy's Question Corner

Cnart your growth and progress using Quizzy's Question Corner. Select your age group on the right hand side and begin to answer questions!
Record your scores for each day you play and see how much you improve!

Date	Total Questions you have tried	Total Score and Kinz Cash Winnings	Average Score per Question out of 5

And in REAL life?

Choose one of your pets to research. Your job is to create a profile of this animal in REAL life! Search online to create a one page brochure that teaches your classmates about this animal.

Include such items of interest as:

Where is this animal found? _____

Is it rare? Why? _____

What does it eat? _____

Is it an herbivore, omnivore, or carnivore?_____

What does it need for survival? _____

How do you care for this animal? _____

What adaptations has it made to survive? _____

What are the babies called? _____

Can this animal be purchased? _____

For how much? _____

What is the common size of this animal?_____

Why would someone want one of these?_____

Draw your pet here!

Quizzy's Word Challenge

In the arcade section there is a game called Quizzy's Word Challenge. In this challenge you must build words based on the letters given. Once you use a letter in the inner ring you may not use any in the outer ring. The most points are earned if your word ends with the letter given in the center of the word box. So, looking at the example to the right, you would earn many more points for the word CRATE (using C and R from the outer square and then A, T, from the middle square, and ending with the center E) than you would from the word EAT. Record words you find here for each ending letter.

Words that end in the letter B	Words that end in the letter D
Words that end in the letter E	**Words that end in the letter F**

Quizzy's Word Challenge

Words that end in the letter G	Words that end in the letter H

Words that end in the letter K	Words that end in the letter L

Words that end in the letter M	Words that end in the letter N

Quizzy's Word Challenge

Words that end in the letter P	Words that end in the letter R

Words that end in the letter S	Words that end in the letter T

Words that end in the letter W	Words that end in the letter Y

Quizzy's Word Challenge
Best Words

After each round Quizzy tells you what your best word was and how many points you earned for it! Record those to see how your skills and vocabulary grows!

Word	Points

Word	Points

Quizzy's Word Challenge
Final Score

After each game ends Quizzy tells you your final score and how much KinzCash™ you earned! Record these to see how your skills and vocabulary grows!

Date	Final Score	KinzCash™	Date	Final Score	KinzCash™

You Won't Believe This!
One day, my pet.....

Explode the moment and describe for us an adventure that your pet has had recently! How did he survive? What did her friends do to help? What did he feel? What did she see? Why did she do this? Would he do it again?

_____
_____
_____
_____
_____
_____
_____
_____
_____
_____
_____
_____
_____
_____
_____
_____
_____
_____

Draw your pet and adventure here!

Booger Gets an A
Final Score

Booger likes math. To play his game you have to find addition sums that match the number he is thinking before the blocks reach the ceiling!
After each game ends Booger tells you your final score and how much KinzCash™ you earned! Record these to see how your math skills grow!

Date	Final Score	KinzCash™	Date	Final Score	KinzCash™

Where's Wacky?
Final Score

This game tests your memory and speed.
After each game ends record your final score and how much KinzCash™ you earned!
Record these to see how your skills grow!

Date	Final Score	KinzCash™	Date	Final Score	KinzCash™

Home Before Dark

This game works on your visual geometry skills. You need to build paths from the parks to the houses to get your pets home before dark by rotating pieces of the path.
After each game ends record your final score, the level you reached and how much KinzCash™ you earned! Record these to see how your visual skills and speed improves!

Date	Level Reached	Final Score	KinzCash™

Growing Plants and Vegetables

In the backyard you can plant a garden. First you must purchase seeds. Plant them in an outdoor yard. Return each day or so and click on each one you planted. By clicking on them you will activate the tools you need to nurture your crops. Do they need water? Do they need to be weeded? Do you need to harvest your crop?

Each day you'll need to inspect your crops.

Type of Seeds Planted	How Many Days to Grow

Choose three types of seeds to plant. Each day you need to inspect your plants and care for them with the directions given. If you let them go too long, they may dry up or get too many weeds. If it tells you to "Dig" then you have to start all over!

On the next page create daily logs for each of the crops you planted. Keep track of what you had to do to care for each one for each day. Finally, record what you were able to harvest for your pet. Your pet is much happier when you feed him or her farm-fresh homegrown food plus you save on the groceries you have to buy!

Create daily logs for each of the crops you planted below. Keep track of what you had to do to care for each one for each day.

Finally, record what you were able to harvest for your pet. Your pet is much happier when you feed him or her farm-fresh homegrown food plus you save on the groceries you have to buy!

Webkinz™ Theater

The Webkinz™ pets aren't really puppets, but it would be possible for them to put on a spectacular production! With a friend or two, create a story map with all of the elements of your play. Then, take that story map and create a script for your Webkinz™ production. Practice, and then share with your friends and family!

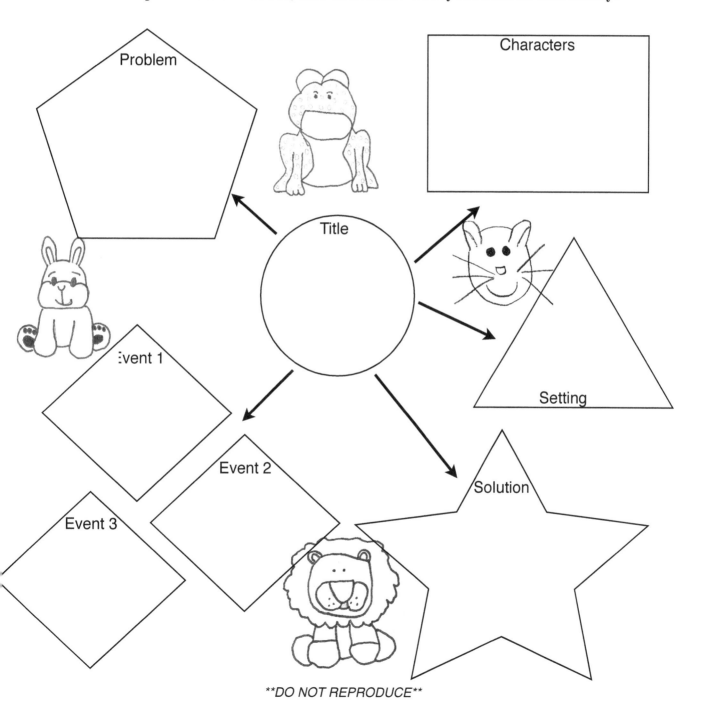

Problem

Characters

Title

Setting

Event 1

Event 2

Event 3

Solution

Webkinz™ Theater

Using the story map you have made, create a script for your Webkinz™ production. Practice, and then share with your friends and family!

_____
_____
_____
_____
_____
_____
_____
_____
_____
_____
_____
_____
_____
_____
_____
_____
_____
_____
_____
_____
_____
_____
_____
_____
_____
_____
_____
_____

Webkinz™ Theater
Continued

_____
_____
_____
_____
_____
_____
_____
_____
_____
_____
_____
_____
_____
_____
_____
_____
_____
_____
_____
_____
_____
_____
_____
_____
_____

Do you have an idea for another activity that could be fun for kids?

Enter your activity idea at:
http://playingwithwebkinz.com

If your idea is used in Volume 2 you will win a free copy!

Look for other products available and sign up for an email list that will alert you to new products available at
http://theoriginalgadgetgirl.com

Other sites from
The Original Gadget Girl:

http://twistedalphabet.com

http://turningtoysintotools.com